St. Michaels, Oxford, and the Talbot County Bayside

James Tigner, Jr.

Schiffer Publishing Ltd®

4880 Lower Valley Road   Atglen, Pennsylvania 19310

Acknowledgment and Dedication

A special thank you goes to Mary Katz, a long time friend in the postcard world. Upon learning that I was working on this book, Mary graciously offered up a large handful of related postcards, twenty of which were eventually used.

This book is affectionately dedicated to my daughter, Elizabeth – live, grow, learn, and give.

Other Schiffer Books by James Tigner, Jr.
Yesterday on the Chesapeake Bay

Other Schiffer Books on Related Subjects
Greetings from Havre de Grace, by Craig David and Mary L. Martin
Greetings from Annapolis, by Mary L. Martin and Nathaniel Wolfgang-Price
Wading and Shore Birds of the Atlantic Coast, by Roger S. Everett
Upper Chesapeake Bay Decoys and Their Makers, by David and Joan Hagan

Copyright © 2007 by James Tigner, Jr.
Library of Congress Control Number: 2007924190

Covers and book designed by: Bruce Waters
Type set in Zapf Humanist Demi BT/Souvenir Lt BT

ISBN: 978-0-7643-2708-7
Printed in China

Published by Schiffer Publishing Ltd.
4880 Lower Valley Road
Atglen, PA 19310
Phone: (610) 593-1777; Fax: (610) 593-2002
E-mail: Info@schifferbooks.com

For the largest selection of fine reference books on this and related subjects, please visit our web site at **www.schifferbooks.com**
We are always looking for people to write books on new and related subjects. If you have an idea for a book please contact us at the above address.

This book may be purchased from the publisher.
Include $3.95 for shipping.
Please try your bookstore first.
You may write for a free catalog.

In Europe, Schiffer books are distributed by
Bushwood Books
6 Marksbury Ave.
Kew Gardens
Surrey TW9 4JF England
Phone: 44 (0) 20 8392-8585; Fax: 44 (0) 20 8392-9876
E-mail: info@bushwoodbooks.co.uk
Website: www.bushwoodbooks.co.uk
Free postage in the U.K., Europe; air mail at cost.

All photographs used in the Introduction taken by the author.

Contents

Introduction

Geographic and Historical Overview

Located on Maryland's Eastern Shore in Talbot County and west of Easton is an area where man, land, and water have for generations coexisted. The area is bounded by the Eastern Bay and the Miles River to the north, the Choptank River to the south, and the Chesapeake Bay to the west. It's an area laced and dissected, carved and defined, and seemingly overly blessed by numerous twisting and meandering creeks and coves. This area is Talbot County's bayside and includes the incorporated towns of Oxford, located near the mouth of the Tred Avon River, and St. Michaels, located on the Miles River.

Oxford was the first town established on the Talbot County bayside. The site for the town was well chosen. Via the Choptank River, a short distance away, there is easy access to the Chesapeake Bay. The pre-revolutionary port at Oxford was busy with the coming and going of ships and active in trade. The exact year when Oxford began to take on the appearance of a town center is not known. However, records suggest that it could have been as early as 1668. Today, Oxford is primarily residential. The town has several upscale restaurants that serve up local seafood fare and there are a number of boatyards located on Town Creek that cater primarily to the recreational, weekend boater.

The town of St. Michaels is a popular destination for boaters and is a weekend tourist destination. Boaters are drawn to the natural beauty of the Miles River, the town marinas, and the safe anchorage in the town harbor. The draw of the Maritime Museum brings many to St. Michaels, but visitors also come to shuffle in, about, and out of the many small, boutique type clothing and gift shops that line both sides of Talbot Street. Other principal communities (villages) that are a part of the Talbot County bayside are Bellevue, Bozman, Claiborne, Fairbank, McDaniel, Neavitt, Newcomb, Sherwood, Tilghman, and Wittman.

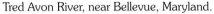

Tred Avon River, near Bellevue, Maryland.

Bellevue is a residential community consisting of half a dozen crisscrossing streets. It is located on the western shore of the Tred Avon River across from Oxford in an area known as Ferry Neck.

Bozman is located on a narrow strip of land bounded by Harris Creek on its west side and Broad Creek on its east side. The community is reached by following the Easton Claiborne Road for several miles from St. Michaels, then veering south on Broad Creek Road and following that road for several additional miles. A post office has been located at Bozman since 1882.

Claiborne is about five miles in a northwest direction from St. Michaels. This quiet residential community has several crisscrossing streets and fronts on the Chesapeake Bay. The community has its own post office, established in 1893, and a Methodist church.

Fairbank is a quiet waterman's community located at the southern end of Tilghman Island. Blackwalnut Cove offers shelter for boats and access to the Choptank River and the Chesapeake Bay. A post office was operational at Fairbank from 1892 until 1942.

McDaniel is located slightly south of the intersection where Tilghman Island Road veers south from the Easton Claiborne Road. The community was earlier known as McDanieltown. Claiborne is about a mile distant. A post office has been located at McDaniel since 1876.

Oxford–Bellevue Ferry, Bellevue, Maryland.

Neavitt is located on a point of land south of Bozman and at the end of Broad Creek Road. Harris Creek is to the west, the Choptank River to the south, and Balls Creek, which branches off from Broad Creek, is to the east. There has been a post office at Neavitt since 1880.

Newcomb is located on route 33, the Easton Claiborne Road, roughly two miles before St. Michaels and at the point where Oak Creek meets with the Miles River. The post office in this small community was established in 1903.

Royal Oak is located at a three way intersection about an equal distance between St. Michaels and Bellevue. Oak Creek is not too far distant. A post office has been located at Royal Oak since 1837. Exactly how the village received its name is unclear, but it is likely that it had something to do with an enormous oak tree that stood at this location during colonial times. The tree died in 1864.

Sherwood is located along the Tilghman Island Road at a distance about midway between McDaniel and Tilghman. The community was earlier known as Sherwoodville. The Chesapeake Bay and Ferry Cove are a short distance to the west and Waterhole Cove, which empties into Harris Creek, is located a short distance to the east. The post office at Sherwood was established in 1880.

Tilghman is located at the Northern end of Tilghman Island. It is very much a waterman's community. The Chesapeake Bay is on the west side of the community and Harris Creek is on the east side. Dogwood Harbor, on the Harris Creek side, affords a measure of pro-

Post Office, Newcomb, Maryland.

tection for watercraft. The community has its own fire department and post office, as well as an elementary school. The post office was established in 1883.

Wittman is located several miles south of McDaniel and is reached by taking either New Road or Pot Pie Road. At the main intersection of the community is its post office, established in 1869. The community consists of about forty to fifty houses.

Early exploration of this area can be traced back several hundred years. For millennia, there had been only the water, the land, the forest, and the Indian. In the summer of 1608, however, Captain John Smith and a small crew of fourteen men made two exploratory trips up the Chesapeake from the colony at Jamestown, Virginia, in an open 30 foot boat. On his first trip, Smith may have made it as far as the Patapsco River, but on his second trip he reached the headwaters of the Bay. For most of his two trips he hugged the western shore of the Chesapeake. From the western shore,

Early morning on Oak Creek, Newcomb, Maryland.

Oyster tongs, Neavitt, Maryland.

it is probable that Smith and his men gazed across the Chesapeake and saw the tree tops and faint shores of Poplar, Tilghman, Sharps, or Kent Island. On a map Smith prepared from his observations, he has what he called the "Winstone Isles" labeled in their vicinity.

It wasn't until 1631—when William Claiborne, a strong willed Englishman and adventurer out of Virginia, established a trading post (fort) at the southern end of Kent Island—that any interest was given to the area. History records that a scant three years later his men were clearing land on Poplar Island off of Choptank Island (Tilghman Island) in what was later to become a part of Talbot County.

Indians no doubt were an impediment and real danger to the early settlers. In 1637, Indians raided and killed the family and servants of Richard Thompson, who had settled on Poplar Island. Thompson was away from the island when the tragic event happened and escaped the slaughter. One hurdle to colonization was passed when a peace treaty was signed with the Indians in 1650.

Trade with the English and Europeans was important to the early colonists. Tobacco, grains, hides, and woods were some of the major exports. Salt, tools, hardware, and clothing were important imports. Shipbuilding was the major industry of the Talbot County bayside. Large, ocean going schooners and sloops as well as Chesapeake Bay watercraft were built. The fabled Baltimore Clipper ships were built at St. Michaels up until the time of the War of 1812. By the mid 1800s, the local supplies of white oak, cedar, and pine had been depleted to a point that building large ships was no longer practical. Also, seafood harvesting, primarily the harvesting of oysters, was quickly becoming the dominant industry of the area. The shipyards at Oxford, St. Michaels, Tilghman, and elsewhere began to focus on this expanding market, building smaller boats like the log canoe, the pungy, the bugeye, and in later years the skipjack for the Chesapeake Bay watermen.

Sidewalk on Talbot Street, St. Michaels, Maryland.

The oyster industry reached its peak in the 1880s. As the Talbot County bayside entered the twentieth century, seafood harvesting and processing were still important to the local economy, but the degree to which the activities were carried out was significantly scaled back. The speed, comfort, and reliability of travel by steamboat and train brought urbanites seeking escape from the city heat in the summer. To them, the Talbot County bayside was a resort of sorts. City dwellers came for the day, the week, or for the entire summer. They relinquished their cares, relished the fresh air, and spent their days lazily fishing, boating, and reclining in lawn chairs. Today, pleasure boats far out-number workboats. The automobile and the truck have taken the place of the train and the steamboat. Tourism, perhaps more important now than ever to the local economy, caters primarily to a clientele that arrives in the mid morning and is gone by nightfall or checks in for a weekend at a bed and breakfast. Yet with all the changes, much has stayed the same in the Talbot County bayside. Many back roads still lead to quiet, secluded coves, and the natural beauty of the Miles, the Tred Avon, and the Choptank still enchant the eye and calm the inner soul.

Notes on a Bayside Drive

Experience for yourself the unique charm and rural nature of this area—come along with me as I take a leisurely drive through the Talbot County bayside. My journey begins as I leave the bustling town of Easton and drive out Peach Blossom Road, route 333, toward Oxford. Cares are behind me and a day of exploring the Talbot County bayside is ahead. At a 40 mph or so clip, I pass over Peachblossom Creek and then Trippe Creek. Forest, field, and farm unfold before me and disappear from view in the side view mirror. No one wants to follow a sightseer; cars and trucks pass as quickly as they can. I eat their dust and exhaust. Demanding my overly curious attention are long, tree shaded driveways marked off with fancy and very estate looking signs. I wonder, as everyone else must, what waits down at the other end of those driveways—a colonial waterfront home, a country estate, perhaps more than one barking dog.

Workboat at rest, Newcomb, Maryland.

As Oxford comes into view, the road bends to the right. Slowing down, I am able to look to my left just long enough to notice the Oxford Inn. A split second decision is made to turn into the parking lot area on the right. There are a good number of empty parking spaces, but the sign on the pole reads "Notice Commercial Waterman Parking Only." Seeing no one around, surmising the slowness of the day and needing to stretch, I elect to linger for a few moments. Camera in hand, I take several pictures of the two rows of boats that offer a mixture of work and pleasure craft. On my way again, I pass the town's tree-shaded park on the left. The park is bounded by the building that houses Tred Avon Yacht Sales on its left and by a small church on its right. I reach the end of the broad and tree-lined Morris Street. It occurs to me that the town would be a good candidate for a next Williamsburg. To my right, rooted deep in the town's identity and praised for its crab cakes by Michener, is the Robert Morris Inn. The ferryboat dock is straight ahead a hundred feet or so. I turn right onto the road called "The Strand." This is a spot well known for its commanding panoramic vista of the Tred Avon River. I have the view all to myself for a moment, then a car comes up behind me and I drive on. I take the time to meander in my vehicle down several of Oxford's narrow side streets and take special note of the marinas along Town Creek. I am left with the impression that there is more want for use of space, than there is space in the town of Oxford.

Town Creek, Oxford, Maryland.

It's onto the Tred Avon Ferry, for a three-quarter-of-a mile-ride across the River. The ferryboat holds six cars, but my vehicle is the only one on this trip. I put the emergency brake on and step over to the rail of the boat. The white clouds and blue sky are the icing on the cake of what is a beautiful morning in Talbot County. Looking toward the ferryboat's pilot house, I notice that the ferry is appropriately named *Talbot*. In roughly ten minutes I am on the other side of the river. I am directed off the ferry with a few polished hand signals of a ferry worker. Driving down the dock, I pass half a dozen or so workboats and the boat launching area.

Robert Morris Inn, Oxford, Maryland.

Calm waters on Tilghman Creek, Claiborne, Maryland.

I am just beyond the little community of Bellevue when I decide to turn around for a quick look. The community is entirely residential with one church in the middle. Many of its houses date to the turn of the twentieth century and are painted white. Some of the houses are well tended and others somewhat neglected. Thinking I have seen enough, and anxious for the sights ahead, I drive north on the Bellevue Road.

Royal Oak is at the three way intersection. Turning left, I immediately pass an antique shop but turn around in the post office parking lot. There is a stark contrast between the up-to-date and ho-hum looking post office building and the antique shop. The antique shop overflows with character, so much character that the stuff (I call any eclectic accumulation of old things stuff) fills two buildings and spills out into two yards. The owner of the antique shop informs me that she does not have any postcards. Back in my vehicle, I continue on, but soon turn into the driveway of the stately looking "Oaks" on the right. Formerly the "Pasadena Inn," it's been at this location on Oak Creek long enough to be called, as the brochure says, an "historic inn." Unable to get a good overall picture of the inn from the front yard because of the big trees that are in the way (surely oaks), I settle for one picture taken from the driveway of the main entranceway and leave. I drive about a mile further and veer west onto the Easton Claiborne Road.

Antique shop, Royal Oak, Maryland.

Signs, St. Michaels, Maryland.

Up the road a mile or two is St. Michaels. I've already slowed down to a crawl by the time I get to its main street, which is known as Talbot Street. Talbot Street is still the main road; you just have to drive slower on it. Not that you would want to drive fast anyway, as there is a lot to take in. This is a weekday but still there are a good number of people in every direction. "These must be tourists," I'm thinking to myself, "for they all seem to be enjoying themselves far too much to be anything but…" With no desire for shopping at this time of day and having no one with whom to dine, I hold a sandwich in one hand and drive with the other. After passing the very elegant and black tie looking Perry Cabin Inn on the right, I find that traffic has dissipated and the road is all mine again. St. Michaels, busy as a bee, is behind me. Not wanting to miss the Maritime Museum's gift shop, however, I promise myself I'll stop on the return.

Again I am passing long driveways with brick columns and name signs gracing their entrances. My thoughts wander again to what it must be like to be landlord of one of those estates. Passing a sign that says "Emerson Point," I make a "U" turn and start down the driveway. Is this the same Emerson Point on that postcard I got last week? Feeling somewhat tense, I regret not having enough presence of mind to obey the no trespassing sign. With palms sweating, I get closer and closer to the house. A red pickup passes, a man waves, he seems friendly, perhaps he is trespassing also—somehow I don't think so. Just the same, I wave back in as confident a manner as I can, hoping that he might think I am the owner of the estate. Suddenly I realize that it's turn around now or stop at the front door and ask for a grand tour. The latter option just does not appeal to me, so while I have the chance and the better judgment to do so, I turn around. Later I find a picture of the stately home in a history book of the area. Yes, it was the same "Emerson Point" shown on the postcard.

Store entrance, St. Michaels, Maryland.

I'm on the main road again, but not for long. It goes south—I take the secondary road that continues straight for Claiborne. But before getting to Claiborne I detour down a back road a quarter mile or so and find myself standing on an old pier. Overworked workboats are tied up there and a few more are anchored out towards the middle of the creek. I scan the horizon looking for the creek's entrance, but from my position it is not visible. Before I depart I check my map but the creek is not named on it. Later I determine that it was Tilghman Creek. Heading again to Claiborne, I see the sign for Maple Hall. The wide, tree lined lane looks inviting and because I know that Maple Hall has been a guest house for many years, I drive in. A man happens to be leaving in his vehicle. He rolls down his window, gives me a big smile, and follows with the classic: "May I help you with anything?" Giving him the classic big smile in return, I inform him that I am just playing tourist for the day. My vehicle follows his out the driveway; he turns left, and I turn right.

Lazy day on Tilghman Creek, Claiborne, Maryland.

Quiet time on Tilghman Creek, Claiborne, Maryland.

Post Office, Claiborne, Maryland.

I drive down to the old ferry terminal at Claiborne. A little powerboat is just returning to the boat launching ramp. The two elderly men in the boat say they caught a bushel of crabs. I accept what they say as fact without bothering to inspect the crabs and walk over with a feeling of reverence to the spot where the ferryboats once docked. I stand silently and try to envision earlier, busier days. Inspecting several rusting woven cables on a piling, I wonder how much longer they will have to rust before they are no more. Suddenly it occurs to me that this is like a tombstone moment. Taking a couple of deep breaths, I refocus my thoughts to the present and leave. Passing the old houses and post office that make up Claiborne, I drive up Rich Neck Road but stop at the point where the road turns into a private drive. Two brick pillars stand guard over the very long and very private driveway. An historical marker looks as though it has a wealth of information inscribed on it. I focus the sign's words in my camera's viewfinder and push the shutter button.

It's on to Wades Point Inn, right below Claiborne. Wades Point has had its door open to vacationers since the time of the horse and buggy. I am halfway up what I thought was the driveway when I am greeted by a welcoming sign that marks the actual entrance to the driveway. The well traveled appearance of the driveway at this point, unpaved, stone covered, and sunken into the surrounding terrain, is quite pleasing to the eye. Proceeding on, I am conscious of the fact that I am treading, or at least my vehicle is treading, on the same ground that has brought generations of visitors before me. In the guest parking area, I turn off the engine, roll down the window, and enjoy the fragrant smell of the many plants and the recently cut grass. The Chesapeake Bay is only footsteps away but I am content to view it through the windshield. Not lingering for long, but content that enough has been seen, I return a wave to a man trimming shrubbery and backtrack out the driveway.

On the main road again going south, I pass through McDaniel without stopping. Because the country store there (named appropriately the "McDaniel Country Store") looked worthy of a visit, I tell myself…perhaps if time allows on the way back.

Post Office, Wittman, Maryland.

On Pot Pie Road, near Wittman, Maryland.

At Pot Pie Road, I turn left and pass the now closed Wittman's Market. The words "ATM, Keno, Deli, Beer, Ice, Gas, Soda, Bait, Tackle" are painted in big letters on the building's walls. I wonder why it closed if it offered so many needed services. Continuing down the road a short distance, I reach the four way intersection that is the center of the village of Wittman. At this intersection is a small, white frame building with one door and two windows that houses the post office. In each window is a well tended flower box. An American flag hangs from the left porch support. A cardboard box with several small tomatoes in the bottom and the words "Free Veg" written on it sits on the porch. A full size, blue mailbox is also on the porch. Examining the various notices posted on the door, I think, "That door has been doing its job since before Ike was president."

Across the street is the Asbury Methodist Church. About ten houses shoot off in each direction from the post office, roughly forty or forty-five houses all together. The post office is closed; its sign says they are closed at this time each day for lunch. I linger at the intersection for about ten minutes and take a few pictures. I see nobody around; even the dogs, if there are any, are asleep. I backtrack to the main road.

Post Office door, Wittman, Maryland.

At Sherwood, I pull over in the grass at the spot where the new road and the old road divide. Years ago I remember taking a picture from this location. Now I am back with camera in hand to snap another. The subject of my camera, the long frame building, perhaps at one time a general store, is accented green. The building now houses the post office and an antique shop. Picture taken, I continue a short distance on the old road until it merges with the new road again. Looking off to my right, I can see the Chesapeake Bay every now and then through the breaks in the trees.

Post Office, Sherwood, Maryland.

Tilghman Island looms right beyond the Knapps Narrows Bridge. Before I enter its domain, I stop to take a picture of the drawbridge going up and another picture of it going down. Driving south through the village of Tilghman I stop at the "Corner Market." It is located—you guessed it—on the corner. The cross street is called Gibsontown Road, but as far as I can tell there is not, nor has there ever been, a Gibsontown. The store looks well established and I surmise that a store has been located at this site for many years. The Corner Market sells groceries, hot foods, beer, wine, and liquor. It also has a deli. I stop in and the owner is cordial and friendly. Purchasing a 16 oz. lemonade in a plastic bottle, I am on my way. Continuing south, I stop at St. John's Chapel. It sits all by itself on the right hand side of the road. At this time of the day it is especially picturesque with its white frame clapboards glistening in the sun. I allow my eyes to bond with the beauty of the church for the five minutes or so it takes to finish the lemonade, and then I leave.

The number one thing I wanted to see on Tilghman Island isn't exactly on Tilghman Island. It's Avalon Island, a small man-made island located a double stone's throw from the shore in Dogwood Harbor. Avalon Island and the land adjacent to it on Tilghman Island was, for many years, the home of the Tilghman Packing Company. It is said that the island was built from piles of discarded oyster shells. Well I guess they had to dump them somewhere! I turn into Tilghman on Chesapeake (a new upscale residential community that has the locals asking each other and themselves why they didn't buy up the land when it was cheap). I follow a wide paved road to its end. At the cul-de-sac, I have a good view of the island. The old buildings of the packing company are gone and the island has been reinvented, turned into the country club for the community. I turn off the engine and roll down the window. To a committed crab connoisseur like myself, the smell of freshly steamed crabs and the sound of spirituals sung by a room full of black women sitting at long tables in neat rows as they separate meat from shell still permeates and resonates in the air.

I drive through the completely residential community of Fairbank. The road is narrow and winds its way down to the public dock on Blackwalnut Cove. I park in one of the two designated parking spaces, get out, walk around, look at the view for awhile, sit in my vehicle, and look at the view for awhile more. The water is still, the sky is motionless; a large flock of birds overhead break the long silence.

Backtracking out of Fairbank, I turn right onto Bar Neck Road. I pass a number of large open fields and marshy areas. A large truck approaches from the opposite direction. I have to ease my two right wheels off the road so that it can squeeze by. I pass a sign that says "no outlet" and continue on. The sign was correct—the road soon ends abruptly at two brick columns with a "Private Property No Trespassing" sign on the right hand column. Turning around, I exchange a wave with a dog walker and head towards Tilghman.

The Knapps Narrows Bridge is straight

ahead. I hope that I will have a front row seat to watch the draw span go up and down. Yet that doesn't happen this time and I zip over the bridge and say goodbye to Tilghman Island. Looking to my left, I see the Chesapeake Bay from time to time. Stopping at the McDaniel Country Store, not for necessity but for a simple look around and to say that I have been there, I purchase a coke and leave.

The Corner Market, Tilghman, Maryland.

St. Johns Chapel, Tilghman, Maryland.

I'm on the Easton Claiborne road again, this time heading toward St. Michaels, but not for long. I turn south on Broad Creek Road. A green highway sign tells me that Bozman is three miles and Neavitt is eight miles. At Bozman is Chubbies Deli. Chubbies looks like an old general store that has been retrofitted for the modern times. I go inside for a look. Chubbies carries the essentials to be found in a country store in a country setting—you know, beer, gas, lottery tickets, cigarettes, newspapers, and the like. I decide to get something to eat. The usual subs and sandwiches are choices, but I select their special: cream of crab soup. There are tables and you can eat in but I take out. Enjoying the soup in my vehicle, I notice the old church next door. Crab soup consumed, I walk over. According to its cornerstone, the church was built as the Broad Creek M. E. Church in 1900; today it is the Bozman United Methodist Church. Across the street from Chubbies and the church is the Bozman Post Office.

Continuing south on Broad Creek Road, I slow down when I reach the community of Neavitt. The road ends at the public landing on Balls Creek. The view is well worth the drive and then some. No one is around; I get out and walk down to the end of the boat slips. I count two pleasure craft, six workboats and five empty slips. I also count seven vehicles, all of them pickup trucks. Filtering my way back through Neavitt, I stop in front of an abandoned and decaying little country store. Its front porch is now being used as a depository for miscellaneous things that hint at what must be inside. I try to ponder the store's glory days, which must have been many, and drive on.

Chubbies, Bozman, Maryland.

The gift shop, St. Michaels Maritime Museum, St. Michaels, Maryland.

Soon I'm walking through the doorway of one of the busiest retail stores in St. Michaels, the gift shop of the Chesapeake Bay Maritime Museum. My favorite area of any museum has always been the gift shop. This one is located right outside the museum so you don't have to pay an entrance fee if you want to visit the shop alone. My favorite area of this favorite area is the book area. I make a selection, a magazine, then wander through the ship model area, the clothing area, and the toy area. Paying for my modest purchase, I ask the clerk what the number one selling item in the shop is. Without hesitation, she points toward a rack just inside the door and says, "postcards." I'm not surprised, and with that I am on my way.

Daylight is beginning to fade. I end my day of exploration on grounds long ago set aside for eternal rest—the Oxford Cemetery. It's nestled up against the opposite side of Broad Creek from Oxford...a more beautiful and tranquil location for memorials to the dead could not have been chosen. I find the earliest part of the cemetery. Without difficulty, I locate the tombstones of a number of Oxford's more notable citizens. I tip my hat, offer up a short prayer, reach down to tie a shoelace, take a last look across the creek to Oxford disappearing in the dusk, and head towards Easton.

The Collecting and Valuing of Postcards

The pricing of vintage postcards is affected by three major factors: demand, condition, and rarity. The most important of these factors is demand. Rare postcards with little or no demand generally remain unsold and their prices are low. Postcards that have severely bent corners, tears along their edges, are heavily soiled, or have had their edges trimmed for whatever reason always demand a much lower price than those in top notch condition.

As a postcard dealer, I am often asked which is worth more or is more desirable—a postcard that has been sent through the mail or an unused example. All other things being equal, if it's a local view postcard (the type illustrating this book), it really makes no difference and the value is the same. However, and it's a big however, if the postcard sent through the mail was sent by an important person, has a message that mirrors the local history that the postcard represents, or has an unusual or scarce postmark, it can be worth considerably more than the unused example.

The pricing of postcards is very subjective. The price asked for a particular postcard can vary greatly from postcard dealer to postcard dealer. The price that the dealer ends up putting on a postcard is determined by a number of factors. The dealer takes into consideration what he had to pay to obtain the postcard, what condition he thinks it is in, how easily he could get another one, and how often he has seen the particular postcard or similar ones. The dealer thinks about the market he has for the postcard. He asks himself, would more than one person be interested, is it a hot item or a real tough sell? He weighs everything in his head and comes up with a price that is not so low that another dealer will quickly buy it and not so high that collectors will shy away from it.

The demand for local view postcards is very regional. Most collectors live in the same state or the same part of the state that they collect. If I exhibit at a show in northern Virginia, I expect demand for northern Virginia postcards to be strong. Likewise, perhaps no one will look at my California postcards for the whole duration of the show. Naturally, unless I exhibit at shows in California (which I don't), my Virginia postcards are priced higher than my California postcards.

One would think that the larger the town the more collectors there would be, but the opposite is actually the norm. Postcards showing scenes in small towns are sought after more than postcards showing scenes in larger towns and cities. There are a number of reasons why this is true. It's easier for an individual to identify with small town America than with the big city or urban areas. It's easier to feel an attachment, an affinity, and nostalgia for a small town. A basic rule of thumb for the postcard dealer, and one that collectors should keep in mind as well, is that the smaller the town, the fewer the postcards that likely exist from it, and the more individuals who will want those postcards. Hence, the smaller the town, the higher the normal price.

Chesapeake Bay log canoes, St. Michaels, Maryland. Circa 1930s; $10

Chesapeake Bay Log Canoes   St. Michaels, Maryland

Demand for local view postcards (again, the type illustrating this book) varies as to what is shown on the postcard and how well the image is depicted. Postcards showing action scenes are worth more than their counterparts. For example, a postcard showing a steam train arriving at a railroad station will be worth more than a view showing a cemetery entrance. Collectors like postcards that are well composed, sharply focused, have good contrast, and show lots of detail. Postcards that are poorly made, out of focus, etc. are always worth less than their counterparts.

Postcards are truly endless. You will never have them all; you will never see them all. As a postcard dealer I have looked at literally millions of postcards. However, I still cannot go through an unsorted box of postcards at an auction or elsewhere without finding postcards that I have never seen before. The funny thing about this is, just because you or I have never seen a postcard before, oftentimes another collector or dealer has seen the same card numerous times.

Sometimes, postcards long considered to be rare are suddenly found in considerable quantities. Then, just as suddenly, every dealer has them and the price plummets. Eventually prices creep back up as the postcards disappear from dealer stocks and are absorbed into the collections of collectors. With one exception, the four or five times that I made such chance discoveries, I released the postcards slowly over time. I thereby avoided flooding the marketplace and destroying the value of the postcard. Several times I have had multiple copies of a postcard that I thought common, but after selling, learned that it was a step or two closer to the rarer side of the aisle.

Postcards are found with any number of condition problems. Water stains, creasing, ink smears, corner and edge wear are some of the more common problems. Unlike with coins and stamps, there is no established and strict grading scale to follow for postcards. Dealers look for condition problems and price postcards accordingly. However, the collector also needs to take a close look. Sometimes a crease, a pin hole, or a small stain is not noticed until it is too late. Examine postcards in good light and from different angles. Examine the back sides of cards just as closely as the front sides. Always know what you are purchasing.

What is an acceptable condition to one person may not be acceptable to another. With postcards, however, most collectors take what they can get at the time. In my own experience, there have been many times when I have purchased a postcard with numerous condition problems because it was rare and/or the only example I had seen up to that point. Upon finding a better example down the road, I then "traded up"—as the expression goes—to the one in better condition. The dilemma for collectors is what to do with the earlier purchase. Many collectors say they use them as trading material, but few actually do. As a dealer, I am occasionally asked by a collector to buy a very sorry looking, rather dog-eared and beat up postcard because the collector has found a better example for his collection. Still though, I have to think that there are many collectors who have "traded up" enough times to have four or five examples of many of the postcards in their collection, in conditions ranging from near awful to near pristine.

THE PASADENA — ROYAL OAK, MARYLAND

The Pasadena, Royal Oak, Maryland. Circa 1940s; $7

I obviously consider all the postcards in this book worthy of being published. Each postcard tells its own individual story and the postcards as a whole tell a larger story. They represent a time frame on the Talbot County bayside from around 1905 until the mid 1950s. The postcards are representative of a variety of manufacturing techniques. Some are printed in color, others in black and white. Some are real photo postcards, made from negatives and printed on photographic postcard paper. Some are even hand-colored. A number of the postcards in this book are rare; others are fairly common. A time frame and an estimate of value has been assigned to each one. The information is found at the end of each post-card caption.

It's fortunate that so many different and everyday scenes were the subject of the camera lens and were made into postcards. It's fortunate also that so many postcards have survived to this day—most fortunate indeed when we consider what they had to survive: the trash can, fires, paper drives, hot attics, wet basements, and on and on.

Thank you for letting me share these post-cards with you.

John M. Dennis, Claiborne-Annapolis Ferry. Circa 1930s; $6

About the Postcards
Illustrating this Book

The postcards used to illustrate this book are from the author's personal collection. The value amount assigned to each postcard is an estimate only. It reflects what one could normally expect to pay when purchasing a comparable postcard in clean and collectible condition.

Regatta at St. Michaels, Maryland. Circa 1930s; $7

Chapter 1
Oxford, Maryland

More than one individual, having caught a first glimpse of Oxford from the leeward side of a sailboat on the Tred Avon, has been smitten with what they saw and at some point later, came to call this small waterfront town their home. Such it is in Oxford, where many residents value the time spent on their boat as much, if not more, than the time spent on their front porch or in their backyard. From one end of Oxford to the other, the town has a nautical and Chesapeake feel to it. A popular destination for the weekend yachtsman, it is home to a yacht club and a number of busy boatyards. Oxford is located on a peninsula, surrounded by water on three sides. The Tred Avon River bounds the town on the west and the north sides, near where the river's mouth meets the Choptank River. On the east side of town is Town Creek. Oxford is located approximately twelve miles in a southwest direction from Easton. By automobile, the town is reached by following route 333 to its end.

Oxford is one of the oldest towns in Maryland and is found on maps as early as 1673. Oxford has also been known by other names, those being Williamstadt, Thread Haven, Tread Haven, and Third Haven. During pre-revolutionary times, Oxford was the most active port in the Maryland part of the Chesapeake. The town was also an important colonial shipbuilding center. In 1694, the General Assembly of Maryland enacted legislation that officially established Oxford as the primary trading center on the Eastern Shore. It was not unusual for as many as six or seven large schooners from England and Europe to be tied up at Oxford's docks at any one time. The great sailing ships brought the essentials and luxuries of the old world to the colonists. The ships took on hogsheads of tobacco, grains, corn, hides, woods, wheat, and wools destined for the English and European markets.

Oxford's most noted and influential resident at the height of its shipping and trading days was an Englishman named Robert Morris. He arrived at Oxford in 1738 as an agent for Foster Cunliffe & Sons, a Liverpool, England trading company. Morris soon became a leading force, active in much of the trade and shipping throughout the area. He established and controlled a large supply warehouse in Oxford. Everything from bulk amounts of salt for preserving meat to the hardware needed to build a boat could be purchased from this mercantile establishment.

Morris was at the pinnacle of his success when he met with an uncanny and accidental death. He had just departed from the *London Merchant*; one of Cunliffe's ships newly arrived in the harbor. Before he was a safe distance away, the over anxious captain of the vessel, who happened to be in the same launch as Morris, ordered a gun salute in Morris's honor. Morris was struck in his arm by stray wadding from one of the guns. He was immediately tended to, but the wound worsened over time. A week after the accident, Morris was dead. Morris's home, as well as the center of his business affairs, were located where the Robert Morris Inn now stands at the corner of Morris Street and The Strand. It is said that a small part of his original home survives to this day, incorporated into the architecture of the inn.

Oxford's economy slowed dramatically at the time of the Revolutionary War. War with

the English brought an end to trade with them, and the turmoil kept others away. By war's end, Baltimore had become the principal port and ship building center on the Chesapeake. At a time of westward expansion, Oxford was located on the wrong side of the Bay. Also, because of its geographic limitations, i.e., being nearly surrounded by water, Oxford had no place to grow. The town of Oxford entered into a long, quiet period with little economic activity. During this time, the town's population decreased. Its streets, hardly used, became weed and grass covered.

The town saw a slight resurgence to its economy in the late 1840s when a military academy for young men was opened. However, the school's main hall burned down several years later and the school closed shortly after that. It wasn't until well after the Civil War, when in 1871 a railroad line was extended to Oxford from Easton and points beyond, that the town's economic rebirth began. The opening of the rail line coincided with the peak years, or what may be called the heyday of oyster harvesting on the Chesapeake. The waters around Oxford were particularly well-known for an abundance of seafood, most notably, large numbers of oysters. Given the ability to ship the oysters by rail and steamboat, a number of packing houses sprang up and flourished in the 1870s, 1880s, and 1890s. Oxford was at last awakened from its long doldrums. The town's population increased due to the large number of oyster tongers working on the water and the workers in the packing houses. Oxford's shipyards were kept busy building

boats for the watermen, stores opened, and new houses were built. The Oxford Savings Bank opened its doors in 1890.

The oyster was still Oxford's primary industry as the town entered the twentieth century. However, years of vigorous harvesting had taken a toll on the oyster beds and the oyster boom of several decades earlier was but a memory. The next several decades saw a slow but steady decline in the oyster harvest. Oxford's population of watermen decreased as the population of oysters decreased. Some of the more determined watermen made up the difference by crabbing or fishing, but it was not like it had been. The oyster packing houses located on Town Creek, at the foot of Pier Street and at Town Point, were torn

down or converted to other uses. The area boatyards migrated from building work boats to building pleasure craft. The steamboat, largely a victim of the automobile and the truck, disappeared in the 1930s. The railroad, no longer needed, stopped running to Oxford in the 1940s.

Today, Morris Street, which once churned with commerce, is primarily residential and quiet. The houses that once belonged to watermen have been upgraded, restored, and are lovingly tended by owners who want to live nowhere else. By boat, Oxford's location could not be more central, but by automobile the town is off the beaten path. This only adds to its appeal and helps to insure its small town and very nautical charm.

Crossing the line, yacht races, Oxford, Maryland. Circa 1908-15; $8

"CROSSING THE LINE" YACHT RACES, OXFORD, MARYLAND.

Aerial view of Oxford, Maryland. Circa 1930s; $8

Aerial View of Oxford, Maryland

"B. C. & A. Wharf", Oxford, Maryland.

Steamboat docked at the wharf, Baltimore
Chesapeake & Atlantic Railway Company.
Postmarked 1909; $15

Morris Street, Oxford, Maryland. Circa 1930s; $25

Along the shores of the Tred Avon River, Oxford, Maryland. Postmarked 1910; $12

View from the Tred Avon Inn, Oxford, Maryland. The handwritten message on the backside reads: "Walking here is practically taboo, so we have fallen in line and taken to sailing." Postmarked 1945; $10

Flying Cloud, winner of the Governor's Cup Race in 1934, Oxford, Maryland. Circa 1930s; $7

The ice breaker on the Tred Avon River, Oxford, Maryland. Circa 1930s; $12

The post office, Oxford, Maryland. The handwritten message on the backside reads: "The weather has been fine, the moon full, but the fish scarce." Circa 1930s; $12

The Riverview Hotel (Robert Morris Inn), Oxford, Maryland. Circa 1907-12; $15

The dock and ferryboat of the Oxford-Bellevue Ferry. Circa 1930s; $10

Ferry boat, Oxford, Maryland. Post-marked 1946; $12

COUNTY WALK AND FERRY BOAT
NEAR TRED AVON INN, OXFORD, MD.

29212

The Strand   Oxford, Maryland

The Strand, overlooking the Tred Avon River, Oxford, Maryland. Circa 1930s; $8

Holy Trinity Episcopal Church, Oxford,
Maryland. Circa 1930s; $6

Public school, Oxford, Maryland.
Circa 1930s; $10

The oyster fleet, Oxford, Maryland.
Circa 1908-12; $25

Another view of the oyster fleet, Oxford, Maryland.
Postmarked 1912; $20

Oxford regatta, August 1909, Oxford, Maryland. Circa 1909; $10

The wide and tree lined Morris Street, Oxford, Maryland. Postmarked 1910; $15

Moonlight on the Tred Avon River, Oxford, Maryland.
Postmarked 1907; $8

The public square, Oxford, Maryland. Circa 1930s; $8

PUBLIC PARK, OXFORD, MARYLAND

Public Park, Oxford, Maryland. The handwritten
message on the backside reads: "Rain today but
I still love the Oxford rain! I've found a boat and
motor. Having a wonderful time!" Postmarked
1952; $8

THE RACE ON TRED AVON, OXFORD, MD.

The race on Tred Avon, Oxford, Maryland. The handwritten message on
the backside reads: "The water is fine,
so is the sun. We took a sail boat ride
and went swimming also." Postmarked
1939; $8

Chesapeake Bay log canoe race, Oxford, Maryland. Circa 1930s; $8

CHESAPEAKE BAY LOG CANOE RACE, OXFORD, MARYLAND

The Tred Avon Yacht Club, Oxford, Maryland. Postmarked 1945; $8

TRED AVON YACHT CLUB, OXFORD, MD.

ED AVON YACHT CLUB, OXFORD, MARYLAND

The Tred Avon Yacht Club, Oxford, Maryland. Circa 1930s; $8

LOVER'S LANE. OXFORD. MD.

Lovers Lane, Oxford, Maryland.
Circa 1905-07; $12

Motor-Boating on the Tred Avon, Oxford,
Maryland. Circa 1930s; $8

"Motor-Boating on the Tred Avon"   Oxford, Maryland

Town Creek, Oxford, Maryland. Circa 1908-12; $20

The Strand, Oxford, Maryland. The handwritten message on the backside reads: "We are enjoying the hot weather and good fishing and good bathing. Taking a rest." Postmarked 1937; $7

Benoni Avenue, Oxford, Maryland.
Postmarked 1910; $12

Yachts at anchor, Oxford, Maryland.
Circa 1930s; $8

Yachts at anchor, Oxford, Maryland.
Circa 1908-12; $12

Yachts at Anchor, Oxford, Maryland.

OXFORD HARBOR
NEAR TRED AVON, OXFORD, MD.

Oxford harbor, Oxford, Maryland.
Circa 1940s; $8

The Strand, Oxford, Maryland. Circa 1908-12; $10

Bonfield Manor, Oxford, Maryland. Circa 1930s; $8

Bonfield Manor, Oxford, Maryland.
Circa 1930s; $8

Public square, Oxford, Maryland. Circa 1930s; $8

The ferry *Tred Avon*, Oxford, Maryland. Circa 1960s; $4

The Robert Morris Inn, Oxford, Maryland. Circa 1960s; $5

Chapter 2
St. Michaels, Maryland

St. Michaels is perhaps the most visited town on Maryland's Eastern Shore, save for Ocean City. Any day during the summer months, its sidewalks and restaurants are busy with out-of-towners discovering and rediscovering its charms. The architecture of the town varies from the Federal style to the Victorian. Its main street, known as Talbot Street, is lined with gift and specialty shops. St. Michaels has a fine harbor, marinas, distinctive dining, bed & breakfasts, and, as if that were not enough, the Chesapeake Bay Maritime Museum.

St. Michaels is located on route 33, the Easton Claiborne Road. The town sits at the narrowest spot on a long neck of land, approximately ten miles in a westerly direction from Easton and approximately five miles in an easterly direction from Claiborne. The front or north side of the town sits on a natural cove and overlooks the expansive Miles River. San Domingo Creek, which empties into the larger Broad Creek, is located on the southern side of the town. St. Michaels was one of the first areas to be settled in Talbot County. It is believed that as early as the first half of the seventeenth century, colonists from the Choptank River area would navigate up Broad Creek and then to the headwaters of San Domingo Creek to

rendezvous with colonists from the Miles River area. The narrow spot of land we know today as St. Michaels was used as a meeting place to exchange information, trade goods, and hold religious services.

In 1667 or thereabouts, an immigrant named Edward Elliott donated two acres of land for an Episcopal church to be named St. Michael's Church. The church, built in 1672, was the town's first permanent structure. It appears that after the church was built, the town began growing up around it and took on its namesake. The first mention of St. Michaels in an official document concerns a horse race that took place at St. Michaels in 1680. A post office was established in 1802. The town was incorporated in 1805. The Miles River was at first known as the St. Michaels River, but the name was shortened to just Michaels River sometime later. It is thought that this was due to the influences of the many Quakers residing in the area—the Quaker doctrine being one that does not recognize the sainthood of men. The name "Miles" appears to have evolved from, and to be a corruption of, the name "Michaels." Why this same progression of name change did not happen to the town of St. Michaels is unknown. Perhaps the name of the town had been more formally

built into the structure of the local dialect and found its way into print often enough to keep it from being modified.

St. Michaels was an important shipbuilding town. From the last half of the seventeenth century and continuing throughout the eighteenth century, her shipyards built large sloops and schooners. The sleek and very fast Baltimore Clipper ships were being built at St. Michaels at the time of the War of 1812. By the mid nineteenth century, the area forests of white oak, cedar, and pine had been depleted to such a point that it was no longer practical to build the large ships. The town's shipyards focused on building smaller vessels used for oystering, crabbing, and fishing. These boats, the everyday workhorses of the local watermen, were the pungy, the brogan, and the skipjack.

In 1812, after years of stormy relations over shipping and free trade, the United States declared war with Great Britain. Six months later, a British war fleet sailed into the Hampton Roads area of the Chesapeake Bay. Then in April of 1813, the British sent a squadron up the Chesapeake to terrorize towns and inflict as much damage as it could. The British squadron sailed up the Bay and burned the towns of Havre de Grace, Fredericktown, and George-town. By August, the squadron was located in

the Kent Island part of the Chesapeake and not far from St. Michaels. The town feared that an attack was eminent.

All of Talbot County had feared an attack since first learning that the British had entered the Chesapeake. It was thought that the British would consider St. Michaels a primary target. As noted, the town was an active shipbuilding center and several of its shipyards were currently building vessels intended for fighting the British. In the spring of 1813, the Talbot County militia—which consisted of two regiments, each made up of a number of companies—began drilling regularly. A small fort was erected at Parrotts Point, on the southeastern side of the entrance to St. Michaels harbor. On August 6th, the British were spotted landing at Kent Island. In response, approximately five hundred men representing companies of the militia from as far away as Caroline County quickly assembled at St. Michaels. They were under the command of Brigadier General Perry Benson. Several days later, on August 9th, the British were observed making soundings off of Deep Water Point, less than two miles from St. Michaels. Also on that same day, a British deserter was captured and confessed to his captives that the British were ready to attack. Women and children were quickly evacuated to a safe distance from the town.

On the evening of August 9th, the militia was on high alert. In addition to the men stationed at the fort at Parrott's Point, a battery was located at Dawson's Wharf inside the harbor, at the foot of Mulberry Street. This battery was commanded by Lieutenant John Graham. Another battery, commanded by Captain Clement Vickers, was located slightly outside of town on the main road west towards Bayside. To block the entrance to the harbor, a boom consisting of logs and chains was run between Parrotts Point and Three Cedar Point. The rain continued long into the night and a misty haze permeated the air.

There are widely varying accounts as to the events that unfolded overnight and into the next morning. Tradition has it that Brigadier General Perry Benson, fully expecting a British attack and conscious of the rainy and misty conditions, ordered all normal lights extinguished in town. Lights were then placed high on the masts of ships and up in tall trees, the theory being that should the British aim their cannons towards these lights their aim would be misguided and their barrages would overshoot the town. Sometime during the night, about three hundred British troops in small boats and barges made their way up the opposite side of the Miles River. They crossed the Miles and landed at a spot upriver from the fort at Parrotts Point. It was around 4 a.m. when, on foot and following the shoreline, the British made their way to the fort. Greatly outnumbered and perhaps totally surprised when the column of British troops appeared out of the mist, those manning the fort offered little resistance. Most of the men fled the fort and ran back into town. The men that stayed (one account says three) managed to get one or two cannon shots fired into the direction of the British before they themselves barely escaped. Apparently there was serious bodily harm inflicted on a number of the British troops but the column continued its march. When the British reached the deserted fort, they made its cannons unworkable and then retreated.

The British returned to their boats and barges but were unable to enter the harbor because of the row of chains and logs stretched across its entrance. From outside the harbor, the British turned their cannon in the direction of the town and began their assault. Tradition has it that the British overshot the town in the misty, early morning hours, tricked by the misplaced lights. This more than likely was not the case, as by that time the sun had surely begun to rise and Brigadier General Benson's own report following the attack states that "some of the houses were perforated, but no injury to any living being." It is more probable that the well directed cannon barrages from the batteries of Graham and Vickers successfully repelled and discouraged the British.

By mid morning, the British troops had made their way back to their squadron—the "Battle of St. Michaels" was over. Accounts vary as to the number of British wounded and killed; the number may have been as high as thirty or as low as one or two. There were no reports of any American casualties.

A well-told story associated with the battle concerns a house located on Mulberry Street. The house is known today as the Cannonball House. The story is that a cannonball smashed through the roof, bounced down the stairs, went right past the owner's wife and child, then rolled out the front door. There are different versions of this story. One is that the cannonball grazed the chimney and entered a dormer window. Another is that the wife of the owner was sewing and when the cannonball rolled past she was so startled that she stuck herself with the needle. The house, a fine example of Federal architecture built in 1805, is still standing.

The Battle of St. Michaels that occurred on the morning of August 10th, 1813 was neither the biggest nor the most significant battle to take place during the War of 1812. However, the battle did secure the town its rightful place in the history books. St. Michaels has long adopted the title of "The Town that Fooled the British." Well, perhaps the town didn't exactly fool the British with lights placed high in the tops of trees, but the British were certainly fooled when they got more of a fight than they had bargained for.

The start of the race, St. Michaels, Maryland. Circa 1907; $20

48

The regatta, St. Michaels, Maryland. Circa 1904-07; $15

Main Street (Talbot Street), St. Michaels, Maryland. Circa 1940; $20

Main Street (Talbot Street), St. Michaels, Maryland. Circa 1940; $10

49

Main Street (Talbot Street), St. Michaels, Maryland. Circa 1930s; $10

MAIN STREET, ST. MICHAEL'S, MD.

Thoroughfare, St. Michaels, Maryland. Circa 1930s; $10

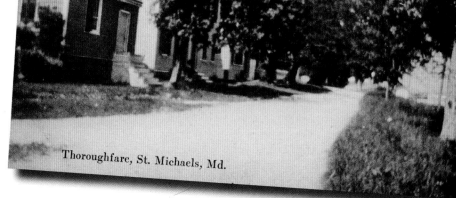

Thoroughfare, St. Michaels, Md.

East Chestnut Street, St. Michaels, Maryland.
Circa 1905-07; $15

Talbot Street, St. Michaels, Maryland. Postmarked 1907; $25

Main Street (Talbot Street), St. Michaels, Maryland. Circa 1930s; $15

Main Street (Talbot Street), St. Michaels, Maryland. Circa 1950s; $10

A parade on Talbot Street. "Three cheers for the Red White and Blue," St. Michaels, Maryland. Circa 1908-12; $35

Mulberry Street, St. Michaels, Maryland. Postmarked 1911; $20

St. Mary's Square, St. Michaels,
Maryland. Circa 1940s; $7

The harbor, St. Michaels,
Maryland. Circa 1930s; $12

"From pleasure fleets to shady streets," St. Michaels, Maryland. Postmarked 1907; $15

Navy Point, St. Michaels, Maryland. Postmarked 1911; $10

After a snow fall, St. Michaels, Maryland; Circa 1930s; $8

R. S. Dodson's Residence, St. Michaels, Maryland. Circa 1930s; $10

Porter Cottage, St. Michaels, Maryland.
Postmarked 1914; $25

The Bridge, St. Michaels, Maryland.
Postmarked 1911; $25

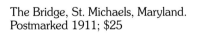

Boats, St. Michaels, Maryland. Circa 1908-12; $25

The bridge, St. Michaels, Maryland. Postmarked 1906; $15

Navy Point, St. Michaels, Maryland. Postmarked 1910; $15

The bridge, St. Michaels, Maryland. Postmarked 1907; $15

River scene, St. Michaels, Maryland. Postmarked 1947; $6

Chesapeake Bay canoes, Miles River Yacht Club
regatta, St. Michaels, Maryland. Circa 1930s; $8

The start of a Chesapeake Bay log canoe race, St. Michaels, Maryland. Circa 1930s; $8

Homeward bound, St. Michaels, Maryland. Circa 1908-12; $12

The old Cannon Ball House, St. Michaels, Maryland. Circa 1950s; $7

THE OLD CANNON BALL HOUSE, ST. MICHAELS, MD.

Public School, St. Michaels, Maryland. Postmarked 1942; $7

62

P. E. Church, St. Michaels, Maryland. Postmarked 1923; $8

High school, St. Michaels,
Maryland. Circa 1930s; $12

63

M. E. Church, St. Michaels, Maryland. Circa 1930s; $8

The Christ Episcopal Church sits in the heart of downtown on Talbot Street. It was built in 1878. This church is the fourth to be erected on the same site. Circa 1940s; $6

Parsonage

ST. MICHAELS, MD., Methodist Protestant Church.

The Methodist Protestant Church was built in 1858. It stood at the corner of Talbot and Chestnut Streets. The structure was torn down in 1962 to make way for a church fellowship hall. Circa 1905; $10

Another view of the Methodist Protestant Church. Circa 1930s; $8

M. P. Church, St. Michaels, Md.

St. Michaels, Md., Meth. Episcopal Church.

Methodist Episcopal Church, St. Michaels,
Maryland. Circa 1908-12; $8

SAINT LUKE'S METHODIST CHURCH,
ST. MICHAELS, MD.

Saint Luke's Methodist Church was
built in 1871. Circa 1930s; $6

THE PRIZE WINNERS, ST. MICHAELS, MD.

COPYRIGHT 1908, BY THOS. H. SEWELL

The prize winners, St. Michaels, Maryland. The handwritten message on the backside reads: "This is the place you would like. Lots of water. Just sailed several miles to get this card." Postmarked 1909; $8

Enjoying a sail, St. Michaels, Maryland. Circa 1930s; $7

ENJOYING A SAIL, ST. MICHAELS, MD.

At full speed, St. Michaels, Maryland. This postcard was published by Thomas H. Sewell. Sewell published a number of postcards of the St. Michaels area. Circa 1905; $10

Summer life at St. Michaels, Maryland. The handwritten message on the backside reads: "How would you like to spend a summer like the fellows on the other side." Postmarked 1934; $6

ST. MICHAELS, MD. — A racing canoe with outrigger.

"RACERS" ST. MICHAELS, MD.

A racing canoe with outrigger, St. Michaels,
Maryland. Circa 1905; $10

Sailboats racing, St. Michaels, Maryland. Circa 1908-12; $8

The *Magic*, Chesapeake Bay log canoe champion, St. Michaels, Maryland. Postmarked 1945; $15

On the river, St. Michaels, Maryland. Postmarked 1907; $10

The fleet at St. Michaels, Maryland. Circa 1908-10; $25

25,000 bushels of oyster shells, St. Michaels, Maryland. Postmarked 1906; $25

Lying at anchor, St. Michaels, Maryland. Circa 1940s; $6

Navy Point, St. Michaels, Maryland. Circa 1930s; $8

Waterfront, St. Michaels, Maryland. The *James Adams Floating Theatre* can be seen in the background. Circa 1930s; $10

WATERFRONT ST. MICHAELS, MARYLAND

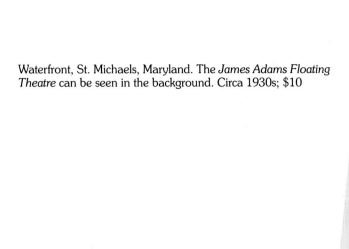

OYSTER FLEET ST. MICHAELS, MARYLAND

Oyster fleet, St. Michaels, Maryland. Circa 1930s; $15

73

Lovers' bridge, St. Michaels, Maryland.
Circa 1920s; $15

A picnic, St. Michaels, Maryland. Postmarked 1906; $15

Harbor at St. Michaels, Maryland. Circa 1907-12; $25

Log house weather-boarded over the logs. Probably the oldest house in town. Circa 1904-07; $12

ST. MICHAELS, MD.,-Log House 200 years old. Has been weather-boarded over the logs. Probably the oldest house in town. T.H.Sewell, Pub.

Rolls Range, near St. Michaels, Maryland. Postmarked 1911; $20

Paramount producing "The First Kiss," St. Michaels, Maryland. Circa 1920s; $12

Lovers Cove, near St. Michaels, Maryland.
Postmarked 1911; $15

Fairview, St. Michaels, Maryland. Circa 1920s; $15

Irish Creek, near St. Michaels, Maryland. Circa 1920s; $10

Cove and bridge, St. Michaels, Maryland.
Postmarked 1911; $15

Sails and motor, St. Michaels, Maryland. Postmarked 1914; $15

Sails and Motor, St. Michaels, Md.

18369

A-1553. Thoroughfare, St. Michaels, Md.

Thoroughfare, St. Michaels, Maryland. Postmarked 1909; $15

Miles River Yacht Club, St. Michaels, Maryland. Circa 1930s; $8

Entering yacht club harbor, St. Michaels, Maryland. Postmarked 1936; $10

Miles River Yacht Club, St. Michaels, Maryland. Circa 1930s; $8

Waterfront, St. Michaels, Maryland. Circa 1920s; $7

Along the shoreline, St. Michaels, Maryland. Postmarked 1922; $10

Harbor, St. Michaels, Maryland. Circa 1920s; $10

The Ark on the Miles, St. Michaels, Maryland.
Postmarked 1936; $12

Navy Point, St. Michaels, Maryland. Circa 1908-12; $25

Parrots Point (Parrotts Point), St. Michaels, Maryland. Circa 1907; $12

Riverside, St. Michaels, Maryland. Circa 1907-12; $20

MILES RIVER REGATTA.

The Miles River regatta, near St. Michaels, Maryland. Circa 1940s; $7

Aerial view of St. Michaels, Maryland. Circa 1940s; $7

Aerial View of St. Michaels, Maryland

Miles River Marina, St. Michaels,
Maryland. Circa 1950s; $7

Miles River Marina
St. Michaels, Md.

Oakwood Park Inn, St. Michaels, Md.

Oakwood Park Inn, St. Michaels, Maryland. The handwritten message on the
backside reads: "Some fish we caught last evening. Was in swimming again before
breakfast and it certainly gives one a good appetite." Postmarked 1944; $8

Waterfront, Oakwood Park Inn, St. Michaels, Maryland. The handwritten message on the back-side reads: "Staying here tonight and tomorrow, watching the regatta." Postmarked 1948; $8

Waterfront   Oakwood Park Inn   St. Michaels, Maryland

OAKWOOD PARK INN, ST MICHAEL'S, MD.

Oakwood Park Inn, St. Michaels, Maryland. Circa 1930s; $10

A nice catch by guests of Oakwood Inn, St. Michaels, Maryland. Circa 1930s; $10

Boy Scouts camp, Oakwood Park Inn, St. Michaels, Maryland. Circa 1910-15; $30

Water sports at Oakwood Inn, St. Michaels,
Maryland. Circa 1930s; $8

Fine swimming at Oakwood Inn, St. Michaels,
Maryland. Circa 1930s; $8

Bathing at the Oakwood Park Inn, St.
Michaels, Maryland. Circa 1909-15; $20

BENEATH THE-SHOWERS, OAKWOOD INN, ST. MICHAELS, MD.

Beneath the showers, Oakwood Inn, St. Michaels,
Maryland. Circa 1930s; $6

Large motor boat, Oakwood Inn, St. Michaels, Maryland. Circa 1930s; $7

The Willows, St. Michaels, Maryland. Circa 1920s; $10

The Willows, St. Michaels, Maryland. Circa 1930s; $8

The Willows, St. Michaels, Maryland. Circa 1930s; $8

View from porch, The Willows, St. Michaels, Maryland.
Circa 1930s; $10

The Willows, St. Michaels, Maryland. Postmarked 1910; $20

The Willows, St. Michaels, Maryland.
Circa 1920s; $7

The Willows, St. Michaels, Md.

PERRY CABIN, ST. MICHAELS, MD.

Perry Cabin, St. Michaels, Maryland. The
handwritten message on the backside
reads: "We are spending the night in this
lovely old town." Postmarked 1951; $8

Perry Cabin, St. Michaels, Maryland. Postmarked 1914; $15

Perry Cabin, St. Michaels, Maryland. Circa 1930s; $8

Perry Cabin, St. Michaels, Maryland. Circa 1908-12; $25

Perry Cabin in winter, St. Michaels, Maryland. Circa 1930s; $7

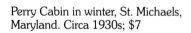

Dreamland, St. Michaels, Maryland.
Postmarked 1908; $7

Ready for the race, St. Michaels, Maryland. Circa 1930s; $8

Chapter 3

Claiborne, Maryland

These days, Claiborne is very much a sleepy residential community. Chances are good that if you drive down to the old ferryboat dock, get out of your car, walk around a bit, and take time to survey the horizon, you will not see another person. The same is true on Claiborne's main street. There are no stores or restaurants; the only business in town appears to be the solitary soda machine positioned in front of the post office. But don't expect to see one of those modern brick post office structures in Claiborne. The Claiborne post office will give you the impression that it's been there, on the same corner, unchanged for years. It's very low key and unless you happen to notice the little post office sign in the window you would think it was just another house. Time passes quietly in the little community of Claiborne, but that was not always the case.

Located in the area known as the Bay Hundred District, Claiborne is about five miles in a northwesterly direction from St. Michaels. The cluster of homes that sit along its half dozen or so streets are just a short distance, straight on, from where the road (route 33), makes a sharp bend to the south for Tilghman Island. When you see a sign on the right hand side of the road that reads "Maple Hall," you know that you have arrived at Claiborne. The community fronts directly on the Chesapeake Bay, but with the amount of trees, the Bay can be hard to see at times. On the other side of the community is Tilghman Creek, which connects with the Miles River near where that river meets the large Eastern Bay. Just to the north of Claiborne is a long neck of land, known as Rich Neck, and it ends at Tilghman Point.

The community dates from the 1870s, but rose to importance in 1890 when steamboat service was initiated between Bay Ridge, not far below Annapolis on the Western Shore, and Claiborne. That same year, the Baltimore and Eastern Shore Railroad Company began operating trains between Claiborne, Easton, Salisbury, and onward to Ocean City, Maryland. In 1895, the Baltimore, Chesapeake & Atlantic Railway Company acquired the assets of the Baltimore and Eastern Shore Railroad and began operating a combination steamer/train service between Baltimore and Ocean City. Claiborne was the Eastern Shore terminus for the water part of the trip and the starting point for the rail portion of the trip. Twice daily the company's steamer *Cambridge* made the forty-four mile, three hour and twenty minute run down the Bay between Baltimore and Claiborne. Once the passengers disembarked from the steamboat, they had only to walk a few steps to board one of two trains waiting for them at the dock. The local train made numerous stops along the way. The express train, the Ocean City Flyer, traveled the eighty-seven miles from the pier

at Claiborne to Ocean City non stop. Locals along the rails adopted two nicknames for the steam trains: the "Before Christ and After" and "Black Cinders and Ashes." The railway service lasted until 1932.

Of course, for many city dwellers, Claiborne and the surrounding countryside was the destination. Having no special attractions other than its rural setting on the Chesapeake Bay, Claiborne's natural beauty was its special charm. A number of hotels and boarding houses were located at Claiborne and also at McDaniel, not too far distant. A 1910 booklet published by the Baltimore, Chesapeake & Atlantic Railway Company listed six different places to stay at Claiborne and nine at McDaniel.

With the advent of the automobile age, the need arose for a car ferry service between the Western and Eastern shores of the Chesapeake Bay. In 1919, the Claiborne-Annapolis Ferry, Inc. was organized with the goal of bringing reliable automobile and truck ferry service between Annapolis and Claiborne. The company purchased the *Thomas Patten*, a 201 foot sidewheel steamer. The steamer was brought down from New York State and renamed the *Governor Emerson C. Harrington*, after Maryland's governor. The *Harrington* could transport forty-two automobiles. A short time later, the company purchased the 160 foot side-wheel steamer *General Lincoln*. With a capacity of only thirteen automobiles, however, the vessel was ill suited for the task. The steamer *Majestic*, capable of carrying thirty-five automobiles, was purchased by the ferry company in 1923. Like her predecessors, she had not been originally built to transport automobiles and was less than ideal. With demand for ferry service growing, the company put the double-ended ferryboat, the *Governor Albert C. Ritchie*, on the route in 1926. The *Governor Albert C. Ritchie* could carry eighty automobiles. She had twin screws at each end, which made her a reliable and easy to maneuver vessel.

In the summer of 1927, the Claiborne-Annapolis Ferry was operating with three vessels:, the *Governor Emerson C. Harrington*, the *Governor Albert C. Ritchie,* and the *Majestic*. Six trips were being made each way on a daily basis. Ferryboats simultaneously left their docks at each end of the nineteen-mile route at 8 a.m., 11 a.m., 1 p.m., 3 p.m., 5 p.m., and 7 p.m. Those riding the ferryboat to Claiborne could connect with bus lines for Easton, Cambridge, Salisbury, and other points. Those leaving Annapolis at 8 a.m. and 3 p.m. could connect with the Baltimore, Chesapeake & Atlantic Railroad train for Ocean City. Finally, in 1929, the company's first vessel built specifically for the ferry company was placed in service. This was the 215 foot, double ended, propeller driven, diesel powered vessel named *John M. Dennis*. At the time, the *Dennis* was the biggest diesel powered ferryboat in the United States. The vessel had three decks, a speed of about eighteen miles per hour, and the capacity to carry one hundred automobiles on its first deck.

The popularity of the ferry service continued to grow. By the end of the 1920s, even with three vessels making the crossing, it was not unusual to have automobiles backed up on the road at Claiborne until after midnight. In 1930, the company opened a new terminal at Matapeake on Kent Island in Queen Anne's County. Matapeake was a straight shot and only 7.5 miles across the Bay from Annapolis. The old route between Annapolis and Claiborne remained in service until May of 1938. At that time, the company initiated a new 3.5 mile route between Romancoke, at the southern tip of Kent Island, and Claiborne. This meant that those making the trip between Annapolis and Claiborne had to take two ferryboat rides and also drive the short distance between Matapeake and Romancoke. For the benefit of pedestrians, bus transportation was provided by the ferry company between Matapeake and Romancoke. In 1938, six trips were being made each way between Romancoke and Claiborne. The two ferry routes were purchased by the State of Maryland in 1941, and in 1943 the western shore terminus was switched from Annapolis to Sandy Point, making the route across the Bay shorter still. Ferryboat service continued until the opening of the Bay Bridge in 1952.

The ferryboats, the trains, the buses…they are gone now. Gone too are the travelers, the tourists, the workers. Pilings that were once part of the ferryboat dock stand silently in the water, bearing a slowly decaying testimony to what once was. Every now and then a car comes and goes or the waves from a crabber's boat wash the shoreline. These days, time passes quietly in the little community of Claiborne.

Promotional postcard for the Baltimore, Chesapeake & Atlantic Railway Co. steamer *Cambridge*. Circa 1908; $30

Swimming at Maple Hall Farm, Claiborne, Maryland. Postmarked 1924; $20

Hotel Bellefonte, Claiborne, Maryland. Circa 1920s; $20

Steamer and train at the Claiborne pier, Claiborne, Maryland. Postmarked 1910; $60

CLAIBORNE MD

Boats leaving wharf, Claiborne, Maryland.
Postmarked 1916; $20

Boats Leaving Wharf, Claiborne, Md.

STEAMBOAT WHARF, CLAIBORNE, Md.

Steamboat wharf, Claiborne, Maryland. Circa 1908-12; $20

On the Miles at Claiborne, Maryland. Circa 1930s; $6

Pavilion, Claiborne, Maryland. The handwritten message on the backside reads: "I am down to Claiborne for the day. Wish you were here." Postmarked 1910; $15

Bergmans', Claiborne, Maryland. The sign on the front porch reads: "Why not stop at Bergmans'. The place to eat. Meals at all hour. Accommodation for guest overnight, electric lights, hot and cold water. Everything for your convenience. A city place in the country." The handwritten message on the backside reads: "This is my home and bakery. House is 30 x 60 feet. Porch is 10 feet. Oven is 22 feet long." Circa 1908-20; $30.

The Miracle House, Claiborne, Maryland. The printed message on the backside reads: "A preventorium for the malnourished and underweight children of Maryland. Maintained by The Maryland Tuberculosis Association, Inc." Postmarked 1926; $10

The Miracle House, Claiborne, Maryland

Steamer *Cambridge*, Baltimore, Chesapeake & Atlantic
Railway Co., Claiborne, Maryland. Postmarked 1924; $30

Steamer *Cambridge* at dock. Postcard was published by Warner
& Monroe of McDaniel, Maryland. Circa 1910; $40

Boat trips, Baltimore, Chesapeake & Atlantic Railway Co. promotional postcard. Circa 1908; $30

Promotional postcard published by the Baltimore, Chesapeake & Atlantic Railway Co. for their combination steamer/train ride to Ocean City, Maryland. Claiborne was the transfer point from the steamer to the train. Circa 1908; $30

The *Majestic*, Claiborne-Annapolis Ferry, Claiborne, Maryland. Circa 1923-27; $15

Ferryboat *Governor Emerson C. Harrington*, Claiborne, Maryland. Circa 1919; $40

Ferryboat *Governor Emerson C. Harrington*, Claiborne, Maryland. Postmarked 1928; $40

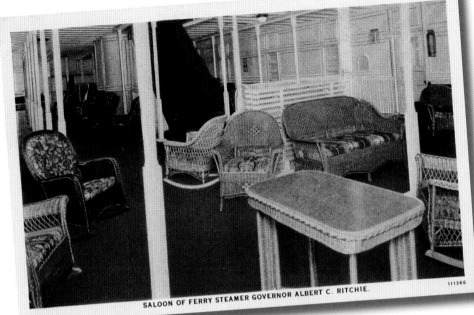

Interior view of the ferryboat *Governor Albert C. Ritchie* of the Claiborne-Annapolis Ferry Company. Circa 1926; $6

SALOON OF FERRY STEAMER GOVERNOR ALBERT C. RITCHIE.

111366

Double ended ferryboat *John M. Dennis*, Claiborne–Annapolis Ferry. Circa 1929-35; $30

CLAIBORNE – ANNAPOLIS FERRY – JOHN M. DENNIS

108

Crossing the Chesapeake, ferryboat *John M. Dennis*,
Claiborne–Annapolis Ferry. Circa 1929; $25

Ferryboat *John M. Dennis* connecting the eastern and
western shores of Maryland. Circa 1930s; $15

A-11 —Annapolis-Claiborne Ferry, Crossing Chesapeake Bay, Annapolis, Md.

OB-H1389

Annapolis–Claiborne Ferry, crossing the Chesapeake Bay. The printed message on the backside reads: "Annapolis-Claiborne Ferry is state owned and operated. It's delightful and refreshing to cross the Chesapeake Bay on these ferries, plying between Annapolis and the eastern shore of Maryland." Postmarked 1949; $6

Maple Hall, Claiborne, Maryland. Circa 1930s; $8

Maple Hall, Claiborne, Maryland. Circa 1940s; $10

111

Maple Hall Farm, Claiborne, Maryland. Circa 1930s; $10

Maple Hall, Claiborne, Maryland. Circa 1950s; $8

Maple Hall, Claiborne, Maryland. Circa 1930s; $8

Maple Hall, Claiborne, Maryland. Circa 1930s; $8

113

Chapter 4
Tilghman Island, Maryland

Some think of Tilghman Island as one of the more remote, out of the way locations on Maryland's Eastern Shore. To others, the island is the center of the universe. If you are an avid fisherman, you no doubt lean toward the latter. It just depends on one's interest and perspective. Tilghman Island has been home to generations of men who have made their living working the water. Fishing, crabbing, and oystering are still the mainstays of the island's economy.

Tilghman Island is located in the area known as the Bay Hundred District of Talbot County. The island sits at the bottom of a long neck of land that fronts directly on the Chesapeake Bay. It is separated from the mainland at its northern end by a narrow waterway known as the Knapps Narrows. The Knapps Narrows Bridge facilitates traffic to and from the island. Tilghman Island is roughly 2.5 miles long and averages a little more than a half mile wide. At one area, towards its southern end, the island is

roughly one mile across. The entire island comprises approximately twelve hundred acres. At the southern tip, the mouth of the Choptank River meets with the waters of the Chesapeake Bay. Harris Creek and Dogwood Harbor are on the eastern side of the island.

The island's center of activity is the village of Tilghman, which starts right as you enter the island from the Knapps Narrows Bridge. Mostly residential, Tilghman is the home of many of the island's watermen. Tilghman has its own post office, elementary school, and fire department. The very small village of Avalon was once located directly below Tilghman, near where Wharf Road meets with the main road. The name Avalon is still found listed on some modern maps, but the village has lost its own identity in recent years and is now considered a part of Tilghman. Avalon Island, a small, man-made island of oyster shells, is located a short distance offshore in Dogwood Harbor. The Tilghman Packing Company (1897-1975)

as well as the Avalon post office (1900-1965) were once located on the island. Today Avalon Island is home to the "Tilghman on Chesapeake Yacht Club." The village of Fairbank is located at the southern end of Tilghman Island. Fairbank, a favorite home to watermen past and present, sits on Blackwalnut Cove. The cove affords a measure of protection for both work and pleasure craft, yet allows easy access to the Choptank River and the Chesapeake.

The advantages of this island were well known to the Indians. Evidence of their habitation dating back thousands of years is scattered over the island. The first Englishman to settle on the island, then known as Great Choptank Island, was Seth Foster; he arrived in 1656 or thereabouts. After Foster's death, the island passed through a succession of owners. Matthew Tilghman, by way of an inheritance, came to be its owner in 1741. When Mathew Tilghman died in 1790, the island was passed onto his second son, Lloyd. The instructions

laid out in Tilghman's will refer to the island as Choptank Island. However, it is widely thought that sometime during or shortly after Mathew Tilghman's death, the island came to be known as Tilghman Island.

Tilghman Island was purchased as an investment by Absalom Thompson in 1838. In 1842, Thompson died and his heirs sold the island to Tench Tilghman, from nearby Oxford. Tilghman's intentions were to divide the island into parcels and sell them off. With the proceeds from his first sale (150 acres for $4,000.00), Tilghman had a bridge built across Knapps Narrows. He also had road improve-ments completed. In 1846, Tilghman sold off his remaining interest in the island to a James Seth. Seth continued to subdivide and sell off land on Tilghman Island.

Boat building was a major industry on Tilghman Island in the nineteenth century. A number of boatyards were building boats like the log canoe, bugeye, pungy, sloop, and skipjack. The first log canoe built on the island was the *Kuddle* in 1856. Two other log canoes, the *Island Bird* and the *Island Blossom*, were built on Tilghman Island in 1882 and 1892 respectively by the renowned log canoe builder William Sidney Covington. Remarkably both boats have survived. The boats have won numerous sailing trophies over the years and are still being entered in log canoe races today.

The Tilghman Island of today is still home to hardworking watermen. The area is also home to retirees and those wanting a relaxed setting on or close to the water. Boats can be chartered for a day of fishing on the bay; bikes can be rented for island exploring, and a good number of bed & breakfasts and guest houses are available on the island. Tilghman Island also has a nice selection of restaurants and they all serve up freshly caught seafood as a specialty.

Dogwood Harbor, Tilghman island, Maryland. The handwritten message on the backside reads: "Having a truly good time. Just live on the water in sail boats but nothing to drink other than water." Postmarked 1912; $20

Bridge over Knapp's Narrows, Tilghman, Maryland. Circa 1930s; $15

Riverview, Tilghman Island, Maryland. Postmarked 1910; $25

Riverview, Tilghman, Maryland. Postmarked 1912; $12

Middle of town, Tilghman, Maryland. Circa 1908-12; $30

View from Dr Wilson, Tilghman Island, Maryland.
The handwritten message on the backside reads:
"Am having one wonderful time sailing, fishing, etc.
Wish you were along." Postmarked 1914; $25

River Dale Hotel, Tilghman, Maryland. Postmarked 1922; $20

B. C. & A. Pier, Tilghman, Maryland. Postmarked 1910; $12

Scene around Tilghman Island, Maryland. Circa 1930s; $5

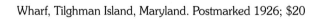
Wharf, Tilghman Island, Maryland. Postmarked 1926; $20

Happy bathers on a sailboat, Tilghman, Maryland. Circa 1909-15; $35

Harbor scene, Tilghman Island, Maryland. Postmarked 1924; $12

Capt. Luther Garvin, fishing parties accommodated, Tilghman, Maryland. Circa 1930s-40s; $10

The printed message on the backside reads: "Capt. Randolph Harrison, expert fishing guide. My catches speak for themselves, Blue Haven," Tilghman, Maryland. Circa 1930s-40s; $12

Capt. Randolph Harrison, trolling, chumming, still fishing, Tilghman, Maryland. Circa 1930s-40s; $10

121

"BLUE HAVEN INN" - MR. AND MRS. RANDOLPH HARRISON TILGHMAN, MD.

Blue Haven Inn, Tilghman, Maryland. Circa 1940s; $12

THE CHESAPEAKE HOUSE, TILGHMAN, MD. :: CAPT. LEVIN F. HARRISON, PROP.

The Chesapeake House, Tilghman, Maryland. Circa 1920s; $15

CHESAPEAKE HOUSE, Capt. Levin F. Harrison, Jr., Tilghman, Md.

Chesapeake House, Tilghman, Maryland. Circa 1930s; $15

CHESAPEAKE HOUSE, Capt. Levin F. Harrison, Jr., Tilghman, Md.

Chesapeake House, Tilghman, Maryland. Circa 1938-43; $15

The Rest, Tilghman, Maryland. Circa 1908-12; $25

Collins residence, Tilghman, Maryland. Circa 1908-12; $30

Tilghman Packing Company, oyster & crab packers,
Tilghman, Maryland. Circa 1907; $30

Chapter 5

Other Bayside Places

The Pasadena Inn, Royal Oak, Maryland. Postmarked 1923; $20

The Pasadena, Royal Oak, Maryland.
Postmarked 1923; $20

BATHING BEAUTIES, PASADENA INN, ROYAL OAK, IND.

Bathing beauties at Pasadena Inn, Royal Oak, Maryland. Circa 1930s; $10
(Note: The "IND" at the bottom appears to be a publisher mistake, as the card
is definitely Maryland.)

Bathing beauties at Pasadena Inn, Royal Oak, Maryland. Circa 1930s; $8

The Pasadena Inn, Royal Oak, Maryland. Postmarked 1955; $7

PASADENA, ROYAL OAK, MD.

The Pasadena, Royal Oak, Maryland. Postmarked 1923; $8

Solitude, boathouses and water, Royal Oak, Maryland. Circa 1920s; $8

SOLITUDE, BOATHOUSE AND WATER, ROYAL OAK MD.

Pasadena water view, Royal Oak, Maryland. Circa 1920s; $8

Shore of Pasadena and Oak Cove, Royal Oak, Maryland. Postmarked 1913; $20

Solitude, Royal Oak, Maryland. Circa 1908-12; $12

Solitude, curving shore, trees & water, Royal Oak, Maryland. Postmarked 1924; $15

Bensons Lane, Royal Oak, Maryland. Circa 1908-12; $25

View from Oak Creek, Royal Oak, Maryland. Circa 1910-15; $15

White Hall at Royal Oak, Maryland. Circa 1910-15; $20

Boats at Faulkner House, Fairbank, Maryland. Circa 1908-12; $20

The Faulkner House, Fairbank, Maryland. Circa 1907-12; $20

The Fruit Farm, Fairbank, Maryland. Postmarked 1910; $20

135

Home with a catch at Fairbank, Maryland. Circa 1920s; $12

Home with a Catch at Fairbank, Md.

Fruit Farm   Fairbank's Md

The Fruit Farm, Fairbank, Maryland. The handwritten message on the backside reads: "Can't tell you anything about this place yet as there has been a heavy 'Nor Easter' blowing ever since we came." Postmarked 1908; $25

Driveway near McDaniel, Maryland. Circa 1910-20; $20

Busy day at the Baltimore, Chesapeake & Atlantic Railway station, McDaniel, Maryland. Circa 1908-12; $80

Post Office and general store, Warner & Monroe, McDaniel,
Maryland. Circa 1908-12; $50

The old Bayside Methodist Protestant Church and the Lowe
Memorial M. P. Church, McDaniel, Maryland. The handwritten
message on the backside reads: "Thought you might like one of
these. We had quite an accident out in front of our house a few
days ago. About 6 o'clock in the evening Mr. Taylor's auto ran into
Grandfather Warner's wagon and mangled old 'Nellie' so badly
she had to be shot immediately." Postmarked 1915; $35

Home of J. Lewis Warner, McDaniel, Maryland. Postmarked 1910; $30

Side view, Wades-Point-on-the-Bay, McDaniel, Maryland. Postmarked 1911; $25

Wades Point near St. Michaels, Maryland. Circa 1930s; $10

Wades-Point-on-the-Bay, McDaniel, Maryland. Circa 1908-12; $25

Wades Point on the Bay, McDaniel, Maryland. Circa 1908-12; $25

Wades Point near St. Michaels, Maryland

Wades Point, near St. Michaels, Maryland. Circa 1930s; $8

Front view of "Wades-Point-on-the-Bay".
Circa 1908-12; $25

FRONT VIEW OF "WADES-POINT-ON-THE-BAY"

Wades Point, McDaniel, Maryland.
Circa 1930s; $8

WADES POINT, McDANIEL, MD.

WADES POINT, McDANIEL, MD.

Wades Point near St. Michaels, Maryland

Wades Point, McDaniel, Maryland.
Circa 1920s; $10

Wades Point, near St. Michaels, Maryland.
Postmarked 1938; $48

Wades Point, McDaniel, Maryland. The handwritten message on the backside reads: "From my 2 windows I have a pleasant view over a fair expanse of the Chesapeake Bay." Postmarked 1941; $8

Wades Point, McDaniel, Maryland. Circa 1930s; $8

Lewes Point, near McDaniel, Maryland. Circa 1908-12; $25

Lewes Point, near McDaniel, Maryland. Circa 1908-12; $25

Rear of Little Haven on the Bay, McDaniel, Maryland. Circa 1908-12; $25

Scenes from Little Haven on the Bay, McDaniel, Maryland. The handwritten message on the backside reads: "Traveling in Maryland my Maryland." Postmarked 1912; $30

View at Little Haven on the Bay, McDaniel, Maryland. Circa 1908-12; $25

Little Haven on the Bay, McDaniel, Maryland. Circa 1908-12; $25

Emerson's Point, McDaniel, Maryland. Circa 1908-12; $10

Emerson's Point, McDaniel, Maryland. Circa 1908-12; $25

Lane, Emerson's Point, McDaniel, Maryland. Postmarked 1909; $20

Emerson's Point, near St. Michaels, Maryland. Circa 1908-12; $15

Steamer *Dorchester*, Baltimore, Chesapeake &
Atlantic Railway Company. In service between
Baltimore and Choptank River. Circa 1912; $15

Steamer *Talbot*, Baltimore, Chesapeake & Atlantic
Railway Company. In service between Baltimore and
Choptank River. Circa 1912; $15

Oyster fleet on Miles River, near Easton, Maryland. Circa 1930s; $7

U. S. Mail from Safety Beach, Bozman, Maryland. Post-marked 1931; $20

Main building, Breezy Point, Bozman, Maryland. The handwritten message on the backside reads: "I arranged to take a little time and come down here to St. Michaels Md for fishing and a complete rest. It's doing a lot of good." Postmarked 1947; $12

Rest and relaxation at Windy Heights, Neavitt, Maryland. Circa 1908-12; $25

Valliant plant at Bellevue, Maryland. Circa 1912-20; $25

Miles River Bridge, near Easton, Maryland. Postmarked 1916; $25

Miles River Bridge, near Easton, Maryland. Postmarked 1918; $25

North Bend, near Easton, Maryland. Circa 1908-12; $8

155

8—Miles River Bridge between Easton and St. Michaels, Md.

4A170-N

Miles River Bridge between Easton and St. Michaels, Maryland. Circa 1920s; $6

NEW CEMENT BRIDGE, CROSSING MILES RIVER, BY MOONLIGHT, EASTON, MD.

New cement bridge crossing the Miles River by moonlight, Easton, Maryland. Circa 1920s; $7

On the beautiful Miles, The Rest, Talbot County, Maryland. Postmarked 1911; $20

Shore view on Miles River, Talbot County, Maryland. Circa 1908-12; $15

On the Miles, near Easton, Maryland. Postmarked 1914; $15

Steamer *Talbot*, Baltimore, Chesapeake & Atlantic Railway Company. The printed message on the back-side reads: "In service on Choptank River after November 1st, 1912. *Dorchester* and *Talbot* are the most modern steamers on the Chesapeake Bay. A trip on them will convince you." Circa 1912; $20